Fairgrounds

Written by Paul Bennett

Wayland

Bodies   Fairgrounds   Light   Special Days
Boxes   Growth   Patterns   Textures
Changes   Holes   Rubbish   Weather
Colours   Journeys   Senses   Wheels

Picture acknowledgements

The publishers would like to thank the following for allowing their photographs to be reproduced in this book: Angus Blackburn *cover*, 7 (above), 10 (above), 11, 24, 25 (below); Cephas Picture Library 27 (above/Lance Smith); Context Picture Library 10 (below/Tizzie Knowles); Mary Evens Picture Library 28, 29 (both); Chris Fairclough Picture Library 13 (above), 13 (below/B. M. Jenkinson), 18 (below), 19 (MEM); Life File (above/Ian Richards); The Hutchison Library 21 (above/B. Régent); Eye Ubiquitous 9 (above/Davey Bold), 9 (below/Jex Cole), 12 (Davey Bold), 14 (Bruce Low), 15 (Paul Hutley), 26 (right/Paul Hutley), 27 (below/Roger Chester); Tim Woodcock Picture Library 5 (below/Tim Woodcock), 29 (above/TWP); Tony Stone World Wide 4 (Doug Armand), 5 (above/EN-F), 7 (below/Ken Wilson), 8 (Doug Armand), 16 (Robin Smith), 17 (Chad Slattery); ZEFA Picture Library 6, 20, 21 (below), 22, 23, 26 (left).

First published in 1993 by
Wayland (Publishers) Ltd
61 Western Road, Hove
East Sussex BN3 1JD, England

Editor: Francesca Motisi
Designer: Jean Wheeler

Consultant: Alison Watkins is an experienced teacher with a special interest in language and reading. She has been a class teacher and the special needs coordinator for a school in Hackney. Alison wrote the notes for parents and teachers and provided the topic web.

British Library Cataloguing in Publication Data
Bennett, Paul.
Fairgrounds. – (Criss Cross)
I. Title II. Series
791

ISBN 0-7502-0864-3

Typeset by DJS Fotoset Ltd, Burgess Hill, Sussex
Printed and bound in Italy by L.E.G.O. S.p.A., Vicenza

Contents

Words printed in **bold** in the text are explained in the glossary on page 32.

All the fun of the fair

Fairgrounds are great fun! They are full of exciting rides and **stalls** where you can win a toy or game. Have you ever been to a fairground? Which was your favourite ride?

4

The **Ferris wheel** can be huge. Some are over 45m high – that's as tall as thirty people standing on top of each other!

These girls are having fun in a swingboat.

Rides to make you

Many fairground rides go round and round. On this ride you sit in a seat like a chair, with your legs hanging down.

dizzy

These roundabout horses move up and down to make it feel like you are on a real horse.

As this umbrella ride whirls round, it tips which makes it even more exciting!

Scary rides

Have you ever been on a scary roller-coaster?
You go very fast down steep curves in the track
and around sharp bends. In the background you
can see a huge Ferris wheel.

8

The round-up is a
big wheel, and as it
whirls faster and
faster it **tilts**. The
people cannot fall
out because they
are spinning so fast!

Bumpy and bouncy

This huge slide has lots of bumps in it. Have you ever been down one like this? What did it feel like?

When you go in a dodgem car you can have great fun swerving, dodging and bumping!

Most fairs have a bouncy castle.
What do you like doing the most
when you go to a fair?

Have fun!

You can win a prize at a fairground.
These children will win a prize by
hooking a duck using a stick.

The coconut shy is a stall where you can win a prize by hitting a coconut off a stick.

When you go to a fair you can sometimes see people walking on stilts. These are long wooden sticks with a foot-rest at the top. You have to have a good sense of balance to be able to walk on stilts.

13

Lights at night

At night, fairgrounds look like a fairyland of lights that can be seen from a long way off.

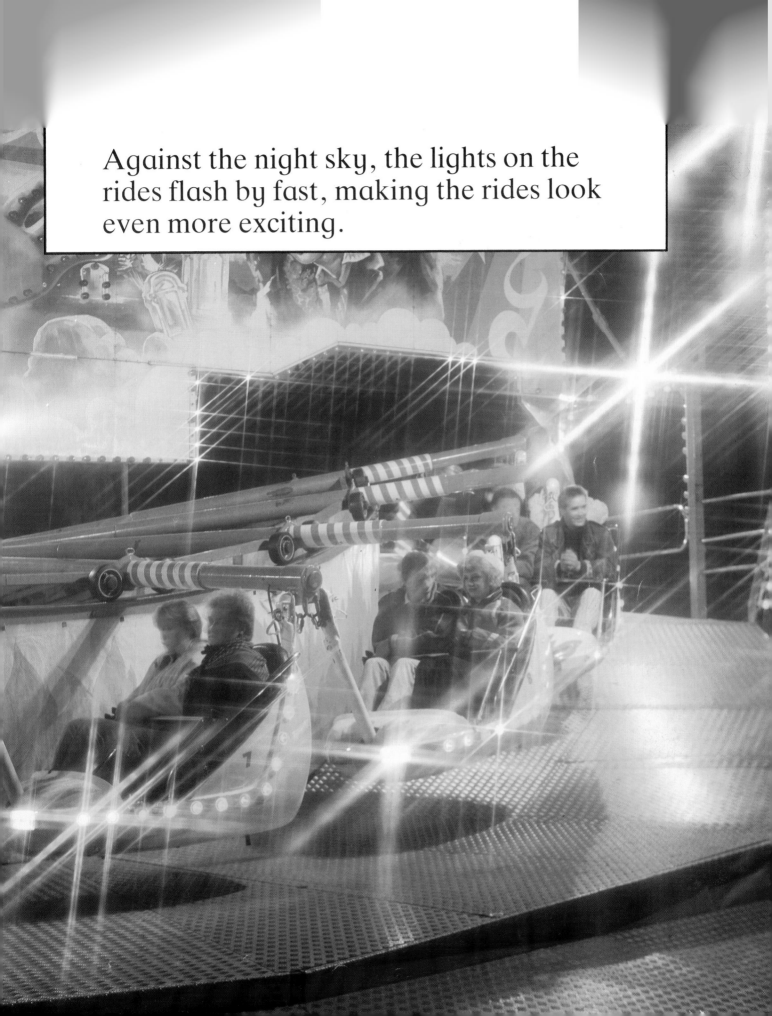

Against the night sky, the lights on the rides flash by fast, making the rides look even more exciting.

Theme parks

Theme parks are like fairgrounds, only they cannot be moved from town to town. The rides in theme parks can be very large because they do not have to be taken to pieces and moved from place to place like the fairground rides.

16

The corkscrew roller-coaster can take your breath away as you speed along the twisting tracks.

If you go on a wild log ride you're bound to get wet! You shoot along in your log boat, carried by the water.

There are lots of tasty foods to eat. Candy floss is sticky, sweet and very sugary!

18

It can be fun to have your face painted when you go to a fair or theme park. Have you ever had your face painted, or painted a friend's face? You have to use special crayons that wash off!

Disneyland

At Disneyland, there are parades, buildings and rides with people and animals from Disney films. Cinderella's pumpkin coach is in this parade. Sleeping Beauty's castle is in the background.

Minnie Mouse, Mickey Mouse and Donald Duck are some of the Disney animals that you can meet at Disneyland.

21

Have you ever had a ride in a giant teacup? At Disneyland, there are many unusual rides for you to try.

In Frontier Land, you can travel in ▶ a train through the 'Wild West'.

At some theme parks there are giant swingboats that are often shaped like a **galleon**.

Whichever ride you choose to go on, whether it's at a theme park or your local fair, you are sure to have fun!

Fairground art and

Fairgrounds are brightly painted places. They make you want to try a ride.

Merry-go-round horses are very colourful. Some rides have paintings of pop stars, such as Michael Jackson.

travelling

Years ago the people who worked at fairs travelled from town to town in a caravan pulled by a horse. Nowadays the fairground workers live in modern caravans.

Fairground history

In the past, fairs had all kinds of things to do apart from rides. Puppet shows, **skittles**, juggling, plays and eating and drinking were popular.

This five hundred-year-old picture of a fair shows people dancing to music in Germany.

◀ This picture shows someone climbing a pole to reach some food.

This fairground ride is ▶ two hundred years old and is a bit like a modern roller-coaster. People have been having fun at fairs for hundreds of years!

Notes for parents and teachers

Language
- Using Disney characters and stories as a stimulus, rewrite these traditional tales changing the endings, reversing stereotypes, mixing up the characters within one story, etc.

Maths
- Ideas for repeated addition worksheets eg. Draw two people in six dodgem cars. How many altogether?
- Measurement. Introduce the need for a standard measure – cm, m, etc in the context of the distance you have to stand away from a game. Also measure the circumference of a circle. (Investigate shape in this environment, focusing on properties of circles).
- Money. Hold a school fair to collect money for charity. Calculate money spent, change, totals, etc.

Technology
- Design, make, test and evaluate working machines and funfair rides from junk materials or construction toys. Also design model people to fit the swings, roundabouts, etc.
- A design technology project could be for groups of children to design a different stall. They could design the posters, work out the cost, decide on the materials needed, etc.
- Children could explore energy change which results in movement, eg rubber-band, balloon, power, pneumatics, hydraulics (eg Jack-in-the-box, hammer and bell). They could design a merry-go-round controlling its movement using wheels, pulleys or gears.

Geography
- Children could suggest and list how fun fairs affect their own community.
- Arrange for someone from a local fair to come in and talk to the children about their job, lifestyle, etc.

History
- Discuss how the first fairs were gatherings of merchants who traded goods. Then how a little later in history, entertainers began to set up sideshows to entertain the merchants. Today the merchants have disappeared and only the entertainment remains.

P.H.S.E.
- Compare the lives of the children in school with the way of life, homes, education, etc of the children who live at the fair. Discuss the different ways of living, ensuring equal status is given to all.

Dance
- Using cooperative dance movements, explore the movements and actions of the swingboats, merry-go-rounds, etc.

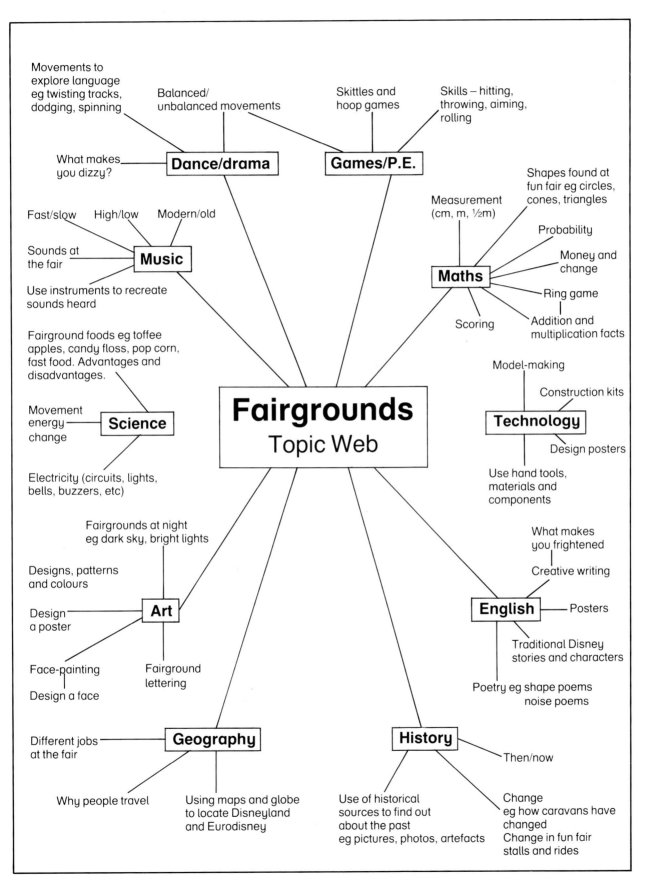

Movements to explore language eg twisting tracks, dodging, spinning

What makes you dizzy?

Balanced/ unbalanced movements

Dance/drama

Skittles and hoop games

Skills – hitting, throwing, aiming, rolling

Games/P.E.

Fast/slow   High/low   Modern/old

Sounds at the fair

Music

Use instruments to recreate sounds heard

Measurement (cm, m, ½m)

Shapes found at fun fair eg circles, cones, triangles

Probability

Money and change

Maths

Ring game

Scoring

Addition and multiplication facts

Fairground foods eg toffee apples, candy floss, pop corn, fast food. Advantages and disadvantages.

Movement energy change

Science

Electricity (circuits, lights, bells, buzzers, etc)

Fairgrounds
Topic Web

Model-making

Construction kits

Technology

Design posters

Use hand tools, materials and components

What makes you frightened

Creative writing

English   — Posters

Traditional Disney stories and characters

Poetry eg shape poems noise poems

Fairgrounds at night eg dark sky, bright lights

Designs, patterns and colours

Design a poster

Art

Face-painting

Design a face

Fairground lettering

Different jobs at the fair

Geography

Why people travel

Using maps and globe to locate Disneyland and Eurodisney

History

Then/now

Use of historical sources to find out about the past eg pictures, photos, artefacts

Change eg how caravans have changed
Change in fun fair stalls and rides

Glossary

Ferris wheel A large fairground wheel with seats that swing freely.

Galleon A large sailing ship.

Skittles A game in which bottle-shaped objects are knocked over by a ball.

Stalls Stands or booths at a fairground where you can win a prize.

Tilts Leans or slopes at an angle.

Index